Discoveries

An Artistic Poetic Collection

Jerrel E. Wolfe

Copyright © 2022 by Jerrel E. Wolfe

ISBN: 978-1-990695-76-6 (Paperback)
978-1-990695-77-3 (E-book)

All rights reserved. No part of this publication may be reproduced, distributed, or transmitted in any form or by any means, including photocopying, recording, or other electronic or mechanical methods, without the prior written permission of the publisher, except in the case brief quotations embodied in critical reviews and other noncommercial uses permitted by copyright law.

The views expressed in this book are solely those of the author and do not necessarily reflect the views of the publisher, and the publisher hereby disclaims any responsibility for them. Some names and identifying details in this book have been changed to protect the privacy of individuals.

BookSide Press
877-741-8091
www.booksidepress.com
orders@booksidepress.com

CONTENTS

Dedication
Summoning of the White Horse 9
The Heart Is on The Table 12
Today I Met An Angel 15
God's Message 19
Somewhere 22
Crossroads 24
Always at my side 26
Today I Saw Destiny 28
Departing Angel 30
Riding for your friend 32
Each Day 36
Flying With God 37
Immersed In The Light 39
The Road Chosen 41
Growing, Growing, ... Gone 44
Help Us 47
Loving You 49
Men, Watch your Lady Slumber 51
Fathers Love Your Children 54
Recipe for Life 56
My Essence 59
New Love 61
Our Gift Of Beauty 66
A lifetime 68
Questions 70

The Connection	72
I Am The Seasons - You Are the Wind	76
Walking Together	78
Soulmate	80
Summers Gone	82
A Place In Time	84
An Orchard to Remember	86
Eyes of Steel	88
Timeless Separation	90
Time with you	94
Wedding Wish	95
How Noble Can One Be	96
Who's Next	98
Who Am I	100
We Poets	103

Dedication

I dedicate this book to the person who saw the potential and art in the words I write. The inspiration was bestowed by a higher power when an earthly angel brought me back from the depths of a destruction. They say angels walk this earth, and in Benita Sifuentes, I have found the one who brought me back into the fold, laying the groundwork for the Lord's blessing which I bring to you in Discoveries.

Summoning of the White Horse

Throughout the distant sunlight
amidst the smoke and plunder
I saw a figure on the hill
standing there amongst the kill
Four legs of beauty had done his duty
on this dreadful day

I struggled to one knee to see
all drenched in blood in a crimson sea
A pristine steed with head held low
as if inside that he would know
The sacrifice made here today
where on this field so many lay

And now as the light of day grows dim
I do attempt to summon him
With gentle tender motions made
he notices my shining saber blade

All energy drained I fell again
and dreamed of pleasant times
With deep respect
he made the trek
To be here by my side

The warmth of his breath
summoned me
And gave me strength to rise
His kneeling stance
gave me a chance
As I looked into his eyes

From where he came I know not
but he was there for me
Outside this carnage battlefield
was where I ought to be

With gentle steps he carried me
softly along the way
All energy spent together we went
on this solemn day
And with trust in him I settled in
with nothing more to say

This steed of white
traveled through the night
As if guided by a power
and in my heart I knew that this
could not be the final hour

Then in the mist I saw the lights
of a distant sheltered sight
...And thought...
Angel's there with long dark hair
to help me through this night

I visioned her softness
her tender loving touch
Her eyes deep as the sea
a person this steed found
In his attempt to rescue me

I awoke in her arms
and cried with relief
Thanking my stallion steed
and honoring the love
Of a woman sent from above
who was ultimately there for me

The Heart Is on The Table

Lying on the table
with the surgeon in my heart
Repairing all the damage
that life has torn apart

She has me at her mercy
she controls the ebb and flow
Of the life I've yet to live
and the roads that I must hoe

Her fingers must be gentle
it's the dexterity there in she
Not to bruise the tissue
or further injure me

And when closure has been made
and the body has been healed
I'll take the blows upon that chest
her repairs won't come unsealed

I'll have a life back in control
where hope and love is a must
I'll only open up my heart
to the one that I can trust

But right now I still lay on the table
the surgeon at my side
To fix me well save me from hell
with stitches that's been tied

Great healers there are many
and surgeons walk this earth
Saving man from danger
and children at their birth

They have only one intention
and that's to do their job just right
When they go to bed and night
they pray for more insight

Jerrel E. Wolfe

It's not just with the hands
and precision they work their trade
But the bedside manner
for complete recovery must be made

Today I Met An Angel

Today I viewed a headstone
worn and tilted over time
Saw a name upon it
very similar to mine

I know there was no relationship
I... but a thousand miles away
The inscription thereupon it
said miss Jesse... born a slave

In my mind I traveled back in time
I felt the autumn breeze
I fell into a dreamlike state
as I sat amongst the leaves

And I as a caring soul
walked in the past as if a ghost
Into a room with Jesse Morgan
and the ones she loved the most

Jerrel E. Wolfe

—

Tired and drained and full of pain
she made it to her chair
Slowly turning to align just right
she eased her bottom there

A sigh blew past her parted lips
as her shoulders dropped in place
The wear and tear of many years
was etched upon her face

A sweetness still exuded
from her frail southern voice
As she spoke about her children
in a life that had no choice

You see...
Miss Jesse kept the mansion
in its elegant southern grace
Tended to the inside
master's children not her race

Thirteen children she had bore
in her ninety years in this place
Her wrinkles told a story
as I stared upon her face

Taken from her loving touch
sold on any day
Some barely able to walk or talk
just simply swept away

Now in the dimness
of the Autumn's pale sunlight
She speaks into the shadows
to her chillum with delight

There's Thomas he's the tall one
with scars upon his back
George Earl and Sarah
all the little ones around they sat

They looked upon their dying mother
as she gently passed away
Saying to all...I love you
In the last breath taken that day

-

Now
Leaves blow around the headstone
as if children drawing near
To hug their loving mother
and keep her warm this time of year

We'll never really know the love
of a family torn this way
Lest we pause and look into the past
in the dim light of a harvest day

God's Message

God each year you paint a picture
for all the world to see
Now I finally see it
as you stand here next to me

I gaze upon the autumn leaves
strewn across the lawn
Visioning of all the loves and lives lost
throughout the ages gone

In the maples I see soldiers
lying on the battleground
In the oaks I see broken marriages
wilted loves that did once abound

In the quiet coolness of this autumn day
I drop down to my knees
Reaching out to touch past lives
to feel their memories

Jerrel E. Wolfe

Here I touch a young man
who died and left a wife
Now a brave warrior
who battled for his life

Now an Army veteran
an aviator too
Submariners and Navy seals
whose lives we never knew

And to my right the mighty oak
has released from its loving arm
A broken aged and withered leaf
of Victorian love gone wrong

With my touch I feel the moistness
of another ancient tear
And vision another broken heart
two lovers parted here

I see God why you paint this picture

and place me on my knee

There's a message in every leaf

that's fallen from the tree

Somewhere

Somewhere in the distance
a candle burns for us
A glowing light to guide
past all the troubles and the fuss

Somewhere in the future
our hearts will beat as one
Spending time together
enjoying all the fun

Somewhere down the path of life
we'll smile and reminisce
Remembering New Orleans
...our first romantic kiss

Somewhere when we reach out
in our dreams we will see
Two lives brought together
a meeting meant to be

Somewhere in the process of thought
neither of us will want for naught
Our somewhere will be right here
enjoying each other year to year

Crossroads

Between yesterday and tomorrow
lies the heartache and the pain
Dealing with the past life
not ready to board futures train

Sometimes there are no answers
though we search and search each day
Not realizing we must move forward
for there is no other way

We can't retrace our footsteps
or turn back hands of time
Can't patch the holes where love was lost
or regain what was divine

Tomorrow's not tomorrow
just another day in the past
No joyous fun filled memories
...to rise will be a task

So here we sit in silence
shattered hearts and broken dreams
Resigned in melancholy thoughts
life stops..........or so it seems

We can pray for all the answers
but it's true friends we must hear
Realize today is a blessing
in a life lived so unclear

See tomorrow's path before us
as a new life to begin
Ask the Lord for direction...
and bravely step right in

Always at my side

Life is never lived
without the one you loved
they're simply gone away
For to reminisce about the past
provides enjoyment every day

You can touch upon the laughter
the courtship and things you know
Look at your family
and the seeds that you both did grow

To speak and ask the questions
though a dozen years have passed
Brings forth the answers never heard
...they're always in your grasp

Through my eyes.......
my partner's never left me
He's in my mind at night
he sleeps at my side
and cuddles me real tight

There are times I feel the presence
his heart beats within me
Times of quiet comfort
knowing he'll always be there you see

His love is everlasting
he knows I love him so
He's always looking out for me
he's in my shadow's glow

To live this life over
realizing the solitude of years past
It's just a small price to pay
for a love that forever lasts

Today I Saw Destiny

While strolling
through the sands of time
late one afternoon
I visioned heaven's pathway
there on a distant dune

The sun was touching ocean caps
its distant pastel hue
Brightened up the placid sky
to the doorway I could view

I never seemed to get there
though I quickened pace this time
My feet were skimming o'er the sand
splashing in the brine

As breathless as I had become
God had made this very clear
He showed me
that there was a place for me
That my time was not so near

I fell into the sea and touched sand
as the picture faded away
Leaving me with just a sunset
on this autumn day

In quiet desperation
I searched my life and past
Getting ready for the journey
when the doorway unfolds at last

Now as the aura fades
and the sun sinks beneath the sea
I'm left in quiet wonderment
of what God's plan is for me

Departing Angel

The rain gently danced on the patio
as the fronts cooling breeze
passed my tear soaked face
I sit alone motionless
staring into the rippled pool
while searching my existence in this space

The vision is quite tunneled here
no glance from side to side
Just the piercing view
into a love I knew
and an emptiness deep inside

As mortals when we walk this earth
we know not
when God will call for angels
He takes them at his beck and call
leaving desperate lives in tangles

When our love for him is stronger

than our love for you and me

It helps us with our answers

...heavens the place we long to be

So as I stare into this pool

and reflect upon this life

I'll certainly miss the love and kiss

of an angel once my wife

Riding for your friend

My thoughts were clouded
as I went to bed last night
So I summoned forth
my steed of white
To carry me in dreams from here
and place me at your side

I know not why this bothered me
but I knew in you I had to see
the reason for this ride

Seventeen hands high
this steed could fly
His wings unfurled
towards heavens sky

Now firmly in the saddle
of this white horse
I've come to know
I see the future I see the past
and places I can go

Emanating from my soul

a horse comes forth this way

For me to call upon

on any given day

Tonight I ride to touch the heart

of one so near and dear

A special gifted lady

whom I can see through quite clear

This trip not really needed

no emergency in sight

My steed thinks I must be

at her side this star lit night

And now

as we glide from the heavens

I see her in the park

A true and trusted friend

walks with her in the dark

I listen quite intently
as we walk behind them so
Place a gentle nudge upon them
to direct them where to go

She felt it as she looked up
wondering what this sign might be
It was me upon that tall white horse
a vision she could not see

My friend still walks with her
through her life of pain sorrow
Giving hope and caring
both for today and tomorrow

I see no other purpose
for us to be here this summer's night
So I summon my companion
...my special steed of white

We too have reached into the heart

of one who is quite troubled

The number of her needed friends

has just little more than doubled

If she calls upon us

on nights of pain and anguish

We'll glide right there

...touch her hair

...Wink nod and vanish

Each Day

In the shadows of a darkened room
I hear your whispers

In the cool breeze of an autumn day
I feel your touch

In the garden of this mansion
I grasp your flowered scent

In the heat of the sunlight
I sense your warmth upon my neck

In each drink that passes o'er my lips
I taste your tender kiss

And each moment that I live this life
your presence I do miss

Flying With God

On winged flight we fly
above clouds of puffy white
Viewing distant horizon
...there is no end in sight

Gods view of this planet
from 30,000 feet
Is pure and chase a special place
cloud cover beneath our feet

On this day of sunshine
I travel free from fear
I feel the presence of the Lord
as the mist streams past my ear

I think of what's below me
beneath the cumulous mass
The pain suffering and agony
of those who live in glass

For should they never build a life

with God and family

They're sure to never fly above the clouds

...to view eternity

Immersed In The Light

To become one with the sunset
along that Pennsylvania ridge
It didn't take long to realize
for the moment I held the edge

I held the edge over all mankind
for I could in this light of day
Seeing the life that had passed by me
and the reasons that I pray

The aura of the autumn light
encompassed me in its grace
Entranced in the moment
its warmth upon my face

I saw three crosses in the sun
and heard God speak to me
Felt the touch within my heart
He was there to rescue me

Jerrel E. Wolfe

Caught up in the moment
where it was just He and me
I discovered my life's purpose
direction for me to see

He faded with the sunset
while the glow still touched the sky
Left me crying helplessly
tears streaming from my eyes

A power had just consumed me
one I had never come to know
Cleansed my inner being
so my poetry would flow

So now I have a mission
a journey for your ear
Write my words of wisdom
and God's teachings for you to hear

The Road Chosen

This journey began not long ago
twenty years are in the past
The time spent with you
flew by very very fast

Great memories that we've come to know
overshadow all the bad
Our chance encounter which led to this
may not at all been had

The children brought into this world
will plant seeds of you and me
Carrying on our courtship
even when you I cannot see

I had planned on building memories
of a life built just for us
Look back upon them
know our vows were true and just

Though memories surely end right here
with this crushing blow
There will never be a time in life
I regret the you I came to know

Your love of unbridled passion
the feeling of your kiss
Times spent on the dance floor
...those days I'll reminisce

A glove that seemed to fit so well
a loving noble dad
Abandoned and discarded
the angels feel so sad

Here's wishing you the best in life
and find your place to be
Seek out all the happiness
you could not find in me

Know that eventually you'll be forgiven

as the pain begins to pass

And I will always look upon you

as the love of my life past

Growing, Growing, ... Gone

Sometimes in life we are forced
to become more than who we are
To grow up rather quickly
with life's challenges testing the bar

The pressures mount quickly
tasks we cannot perceive
Somehow summons inner strength
from deep inside of me

From daily childhood pleasures
to adult routines I go
Picking up the pieces
of a major crushing blow

I do feel love around me
Gods placed his tender hand
Upon me and my father
who is my only man

There's caring and concern
hugs and a needed kiss
Just the right remedy
for times such as this

The future is quite misty
one that I cannot see quite clear
It's laid out before me
its time is drawing near

And as I prepare to leave
a house that I called home
I venture down a highway
...a new life for to roam

My life certainly has turned
the corner the past two months or so
From realizing where I've come
but not to where I go

Parents can't protect me now
they know not the path I take
It will be me and the Lord above
a journey we both shall make

Help Us

The midnight sky is bright with stars
crescent moon glow lights the night
I send a prayer to distant light
in hopes the wrongs will right

You see I see the changes
thought society
Changes not for the good of all
changes not meant to be

There's less respect for all mankind
rude talk and disarray
Broken families and wanting children
have lost desire to pray

It seems that evil's sure to win
this battle being fought
Choosing the path of the straight and narrow
seems too often all for naught

Jerrel E. Wolfe

I pray again this summer's night
that your desires we will fulfill
Save us lowly sinners
and guide us with your will

Please shed some light upon us
and guide us throughout the night
Bless us with a sunrise
another day to make things right

Loving You

Today you said you loved me
it hit me hard you see
For today I wrestle with that love
and the joy you provide me

There is no doubt I love you
it's tough to say today
They're just a couple stumbling blocks
hindering my pathway

On days when full of energy
those blocks I do not see
I glide over them with ease and grace
of some gymnast that you see

To say I love you in rebuttal
and not think about it so
Shows very little disregard
for the woman I've come to know

Jerrel E. Wolfe

I want to love you fully
and from the bottom of my heart
Not play those games of children
who don't cherish this great art

I know I've said it once or twice
or even as much as ten
Each time my heart was in it
no deceit or liars' sin

So please if you say you love me
don't expect words in return
This fire you've started in my heart
continually will burn

I'm working through my issues
of a life lived in pain and sin
I plan to come knocking at your door
I hope you'll let me in

Men, Watch your Lady Slumber

She lays there slumbering through the night
her daily chores been done
Executive things the hectic stuff
and lots of errands run

She's tucked in boy wonder
fed the dog and changed the bed
Checked on the homework
ironed some then just read

This day was quite the normal
for you just must see
This is a mom's life with so much strife
and tears we never see

She will love me in the morning
have a smile upon her face
Send the children off to school
with another loving embrace

Then tidy up check the time
and hurry to her place
Where she will work a burdensome job
in today's rat race

There's not much time for others
lives filled with too much dear
Herself has placed upon a shelf
her needs her wants and fear

So when you see a lady
slumbering either night or day
Place a prayer upon her
and look to God and say

"I know you've placed upon woman
a really heavy task
Protect her soothe and help her
is really all I ask."

You have your reasons
women work this way
I know there's a lot of cleans up
at the end of every day

Your power is so magnificent
you can create a soul like this
To toll through life be a wife
and live in peaceful bliss

Fathers Love Your Children

It was just a guitar lesson
scheduled on a Saturday
A special time to tap the soul
and send tunes on their way

Twas not long after I had begun
my mind was quite remiss
I remembered my little ones
whom I left without a kiss

Life sure has been too busy
to do such a little thing
Now as I sit on the porch
I just wish the phone would ring

For they have all now left me
the man I used to be
Heartless and too busy
to pull them from the sea

And as I look upon it
a tear runs down my face
There's just no place in this world
for me to find solace

If I had taken time to kiss them
and help them on their way
I'm certain they would be here
to help enjoy the day

But today there is no pleasure
no fun no happiness
For I have failed in my quest
to give them sweet caress

Men please love your children
they need you every day
To give them strength and love and hope
as they go out and play

Recipe for Life

Take a loving mother and one loving Dad
mingle them together showing all the love they have
Bake it two seventy or somewhere there about
pull it from the oven you'll hear it start to pout

This is where your real task begins
where you'll be challenged the most
To add the right ingredients
to ensure you're a perfect host

With smiles and love
continually stir in...
A dose of cheer and happiness
to keep structure there within

At three a smidge of honesty
and stir some honor at this stage
Like yeast it will continually rise
taste blossoming with the coming age

There are varied bakers' opinions
in the mix this tort shall see
Correct amount of education
varies for you and me

Instill some dedication
concentration and lots of naps
Grow this combination
for several years and now look back

It's now the final touches
needed in this recipe
Hygiene and some grooming
and Oh Yes!... Faith for God to see

Let stand this treat
covered with a warm smile
Check it often
not just once in a while

And when eighteen years
have come to pass
Unleash this your goodness
to the mass

You'll reap the rewards of
a job well done
A blue-ribbon recipe
you will have won

Thanks will come
from far and near
But none as sweet
as the child you reared

My Essence

My essence travels with me
everywhere I go
Hiding deep within me
looking to and for

I may meet you in a coffee shop
or on a crowded street
When I open up and speak to you
my essence you shall meet

It may not even strike you
or make you stop and think
Who is this man who walks the land
and offered me his drink

If you get to know me deeply
and hold me in your hand
You'll find an overwhelming presence
It will grab you where you stand

Jerrel E. Wolfe

Whence the time has come
that I part your lips with mine
I'll breathe my essence into you
our lives will intertwine

It is now you've come to know me
you have touched upon my heart
Become a cherished memory
an eternal work of art

I've always felt the presence
of this specialness you see
The need to find my following
who appreciates the essence found in me

New Love

I've never built a love like this
and based it all on trust
Met a special lady
where there were more than two of us

I cannot love like sixteen
when each person was so free
No guilt no sin no track record
or sorted history

I cannot live like thirty-one
when business assets caused some fear
The risk of starting fresh again
...many years of experience were here

Now as I turn the page
of another chapter in life
I ponder how I can accept
a new and loving wife

I cannot love her as sixteen
or even thirty-one
Decades of reminiscence
two daughters and her son

There is a love for each other
less strong than the bond
That we have built for our children
as our lives have carried on

It can't surpass the feelings
and love of family
The one's always there for us
the journey that they see

How do you come to feel this
and know your path is right
Why do we contemplate this love
each and every night

It's not a love of sixteen
or even forty-one
A newness and awareness
of this partnership begun

It's come right down to trusting
this new person you have found
To know that whatever life dealt out
your friend would stick around

This time there will be death involved
your mate will surely go
Leaving one of us to travel on
...in a world God's made to hoe

To love this deep and marry
and do it all again
Will bring us pain and heartache
but not the pain of sin

Jerrel E. Wolfe

I know that we must risk it
this new love I don't see
It's not like any of the past
we each have family

Knowing that it will come to pass
that our ex's cross our stern
Can we be accepting
of a candle that once burned

Once was love unconditional
has changed for you and me
A new love's being formed
with children the boundary

I hope you can accept this
and know that it is true
This has to be the basis
of new life for me and you

I never wanted to marry twice
was three times meant to be?
I know your feelings mutual
our fate is hard to see

I've come to trust my honor
words spoken and loving deeds
When you place yourself with me
your heart will never bleed

Should you come to make that choice
to have me in your life
Just show me all the love you have
...I'll return it to my wife

Our Gift Of Beauty

Life's sustaining liquid
is as blue as blue can be
Fueling and sustaining life
in each poet that you see

When life deals us a setback
the pressure builds inside
The artistry of the poet
is something you can't hide

This ink well that's inside us
fills up and overflows
The drips fall to the paper
the poet's candle glows

It might just be a single word
or maybe just a phrase
A picture hanging on a wall
or an idea lost in a maze

Discoveries: An Artistic Poetic Collection

The message that's created
comes from no pen in hand
The verse is sent out from the heart
where emotion takes its stand

You cannot fault the wisdom
that's written to the page
Or the feeling that you get from it
,,,sometimes love passion and rage

A tear may form and glisten
from deep within your eyes
Fall onto the table
as you let out subtle sighs

Yet this is what we give to this world
it's beauty you can't see
The beauty's etched upon your mind
in verse called poetry

A lifetime

So often said of memories read
as I look back in my mind
These are all happenings
occurring in my lifetime

Just exactly what is this
the time in life we speak
Is it little journeys
in life's time that we seek

In my lifetime as a child
or in the married life I found
What constitutes a lifetime
is it a birth to death surround?

Being that we walk this earth
and the journey is not yet through
A lifetime is just a segment
of memories we once knew

I spent a lifetime with my first wife
a lifetime with the next
A lifetime getting past them
a lifetime with children in the nest

It takes courage to tread these waters
and seek a lifetime you don't know
Plant your essence on the earth
and watch the flowers grow

So when the next journey
meets up with the end
Consider It - a lifetime
and move ahead again

Questions

We are a race of many questions
seeking answers along the way
For all the problems in our lives
on any given day

The burdens that we carry
the stresses that we have
Sometimes so enormous
sometimes very bad

Sometimes we have no answers
to the questions that we seek
If only we could have a chance to look
to God and get a peak

If questions get no answers
we must live with this each day
Knowing that the man above with his love
would not break our backs this way

He gives us much to carry
but only he doth know
The reason for the burden
...the path we will follow

So when you're having trouble times
and their hard to overcome
The only answer is to place your faith
in the one who can get the job done

For looking elsewhere in this life
will lead to heartache and emptiness
A burden sure to carry
...no life of bliss and happiness

The Connection

Hooves tapped upon the stable door
as I went to bed last night
The steed of my subconscious
was yearning for a flight

I took him from his paddock
and patted his white face
It calmed the thinking of this horse
ready for the race

I knew not why he called me
but in his saddle I knew
The flight we were about to make...
the speed at which he flew

My steed does not have troubled nights
he rests and seldom stirs
But on this night of no starlight
his mind was filled with blurs

He headed west you know the rest

Oklahoma he was bound

And to his sire with undeniable desire

...to his home he found

We hovered at the window

peering through the shears of white

And found my special lady

tears flowing late that night

He knew that she was troubled

1200 miles away

This steed of white and his winged flight

would chase the fears away

It was just but a troubled night

of memories love and laughter

A time when one sits and thinks

about life's disaster

The love that reached the heavens
the sorrow it has wrought
The golden rings and other things
this tattered marriage brought…

She rose and walked right toward us
and knowing she could not see
I leaned over kissed the glass… drew a glance
…from her - to me…

The expression on her face had changed
her eyes appeared to clear
I got the feeling there was healing
for this woman here

My steed was floating quiet now
his worries seem to pass
He knew it was to be all right
with that kiss upon the glass

Her troubled times are over now
she gently strokes her hair
Somehow I think she knows
her armored knight was there

Twas but another journey
upon my steed of white
One you might look up and see
on any summers night

I Am The Seasons - You Are the Wind

I wallowed in late springtime
my life was just a mess
You moved me with the gentleness
of the breeze that you possess

With summer moving slowly
natures touch became quite real
Your sporadic clouds did pass me by
as my tender heart did heal

Like a whirlwind you possessed me
with lightening you did strike
Summer quickly passed right by
and now Autumn is in sight

This Autumn stands majestic
in early summer sunsets
You blow wrinkled leaves across my shadows
cool the soul and its regrets

The briskness of your morning touch
hearkens goose bumps on chilled nights
I inhale your wholesome goodness
viewing formation fowl in southern flight

The early morning exhale
shows Autumns misted kiss upon the glass
I hear the crackle of crushing leaves
neath my feet along running paths

You've moved me to this moment
the next step obviously is mine
With winter around the corner
one final wind gust I will find

Moving to the new year
a newness will begin
Natures forces and time together
Leaving history in your wind

Walking Together

There are footprints in the sand dunes
of a love who passed away
A very special person
who shared a special day

We viewed out o'er horizon
and talked of the life we've missed
Danced within the brine
as our feet it gently kissed

Looked unto the heavens...
watched the clouds pass over the sea
Looked into each other's eyes
our hearts once filled with glee

Those footprints now have washed away
I find them in the heart
There imbedded deep inside
painted memories...works of art

For to gather all the feelings
of a love that grew so much
Moved us to a higher plane
one that most can't touch

Today I walk with an angel
once mortal loved me so
Captive of the deep blue sea
that would not let him go

Soulmate

Should you ever lose a soulmate
a heart that you have won
You'll never have an earthly peace
your current life becomes undone

There are many loves that you might find
friends and lovers throughout time
But soulmates are far and in between
the glue that makes your life grow green

You may give your love in marriage
your honesty and trust
And many years will go by
before dust turns back to dust

In that time I challenge you
to find a heart that's true
One that will always be there
and hold you when you're through

To kiss you on your last day
and receive your final gift
The passing of your soul through a heart
that forever will reminisce

Soulmates rarely walk the earth
they're usually found above
Waiting for each other
in the beauty of unearthly love

Summers Gone

The ceiling fans are quiet now
the summer's heat is gone
Autumns crisp chilling bite
has shocked flowers on the lawn

The pools water has no ripples
the scene is quite serene
No joyous sounds of summer
or playful visions to be seen

Misting fog lifts from the river
the trees are not as bright
The sun seems to set much earlier
it lengthens out the night

Time past is but a memory
we must move on from here
A new season is upon us
it'll soon be end of year

Summer is now history

filed and stored away

Stories to be reminisced

on a blistery winters day

A Place In Time

The city street was quiet
with a fresh blanket of new fallen snow
Blanketing the pavement
sidewalk park and trees

The aging lamp lighter steadily made his
rounds despite arthritic knees
He'd tip his hat to the carriage driver
as the sled moved down the street
The sound of dancing bells and
clopping hooves were made by horses' feet

Shop keepers brushed the snow
from their walks that winters day
And children threw their snowballs
in the park across the way

There were lovers on the church steps
carolers by the wall
And I the casual observer
was in admiration of it all

A light glowed in the church tower
and you could faintly hear the sound
Of a train approaching the station
where families gathered round

I pictured a reunion
of loved ones gone away
Stepping from the railcar
to unite on Christmas day

I reached over and placed my present
at the far side of this miniature Victorian scene
Marveled at the ornateness
of this enchanting holiday theme

It was done in such great detail
I could travel to this place
Becoming more than just the scenery
I was held in its embrace

Oh what a simpler lifetime
where true love and joy exists
Would it be too much to ask
to live this Christmas wish?

An Orchard to Remember

The love of 16 on a winter's night
bundled from the cold
Two friends along with us
both about just as old

The hill was long and darkened
no light for us to see
But there two young lovers stood
future too dark to see

Upon that sled they mounted
laughter and delight
Upsetting on the left side
beneath the trees this darkened night

He kissed her in the snowflakes
exchanged their passionate touch
In their hearts at that stage in life
there love was oh so much

The bottom of that long dark hill
eventually came to be
A long walk home just the two alone
a winter's love was there to see

Now as I'm reminded
It's taken thirty years plus six
To pull this image from my soul
and get a mental fix

Yes I do remember
this time spent with you
Thank you for the look back
of the time when I loved you

Eyes of Steel

Throughout eyes of steel I see the world
each and every day
Through eyes of steel I see the world
as I toil along the way

The visions seen are checked and filed
and maybe categorized
Life's to busy to fast to dizzy
to use more than just the eyes

But on summer nights neath star lights
when my heart I open up
I check the scenes with all my means
and view them with my love

My eyes see the world so differently
this kickback time of day
There's not so much clutter
more time to sit and say....

It's all there in the visions
the meaning of this life
The joys the laughter
the sorrows and the strife

There's tears and smiles deep in those files
and children to recall
and as I close those eyes and think of them
I know I love it all

Time to rest time to ponder
time to sit in thought
Why I'm blessed to take this test
to pass it I cannot

The visions seen embedded deep
and memories filed away
What's present becomes history
...eyes rest for another day

Timeless Separation

There are fairy tails and dreams
and stories which some are true
Sunshine days and moonlight nights
and fields beneath the dew

There are years of harvest plenty
and times of little yield
Many portions of our lives
where our hearts have come unsealed

Long nights of pain and sorrow
give way to loves tender kiss
There are times that come upon us
that lovers 'ner do miss

To capture a precious moment
and store it in your heart
Gives strength hope and salvation
to a life that's torn apart

Oh you who have the power
to render a sweet kiss
Lock me in your heart
forever in your bliss

Our meetings may not be many
and time will come and go
Memories of you my love
will be my greatest show

Our time in the city
will replay in my mind
And find a place in my heart
until the end of time

Yes you have really touched me
my heart you've filled with glee
I cannot envision any day
where I will not think of thee

Your smile is overwhelming
your touch it makes me glow
Inner peace is bestowed upon me
when the lights are turned down low

Never will there be a time
when the lights are turned down dim
That you will not be thought of
or your space I lingered in

There's something in me growing
and it hurts being far away
That I cannot spend some
special time with you
each and every day

The hours will pass slowly
the days drag on and on
I know that special night will come
when we can dance again to our song

For to hold you is so precious
to love you is so grand
The peace I found being with you
is placing my heart in your hand

So until the opportunity calls us
to be together again
Please know that you'll be thought of
before each day shall end

Time with you

The nights have become quite lonely...
the smell of you has gone
The touch of your hand the warmth of your kiss
have faded for too long...

The intent of life is questioned here
as I sit and think all day
Of the one who reached into my soul
and stole my heart this way

looking back......
The beauty of your movement...
the way your body flows
Your entrance into a room
transcends the candles glow

Wedding Wish

May I wake up in your arms every morning
May I fall asleep in your arms every night
May I be in your arms on my death bed
Look into your loving eyes
and say I love you
with my final breath
Press my lips to yours
and have my soul
pass through your heart
on its way to heaven

How Noble Can One Be

There are souls and there are good souls
winners and losers
Men who strive to win a fight
drunks and just plain boozers

People who don't really give a damn
others who do all they can
Some who stay awake all night
striving to do what's right

We all have a chance to choose
who to align ourselves with in this life
To choose a path of righteousness
or ignore the pain and strife

Though we might not be judged by our peers
as to why we do what we do
They see it in their hearts
the good deeds shine right through

You can slave your life away today
doing all that is required
Earn the cash take out the trash
keep busy till your tired

But one thing you can't do
if your heart is not in this
To gain admiration
for the lives you opt to kiss

If I had a chance to impart on you
the message of this note
Take the time to make a difference
and not do what floats your boat

Who's Next

Have you ever stopped to reason why
Some people live while others die

The righteous good natured people who care
Often taken from this earth…it doesn't seem fair

While others fail and avoid the risk
Forget to love forget to kiss
No hugs no caring no heavenly bliss
no thank you's respect or tenderness

Yet they travel down our highway
interacting with you and me
Sucking up our acts of kindness
and all things selfishly

Perhaps they're here just as a test
To find out where we stand
We the good souls of this world
who eagerly extend a hand

When a good soul is taken
from our lives of disarray
We mourn the fact we've lost all that
...their touch that came our way

It's so often hard to ponder
why God takes and chooses so
As mortals we will never know why
...just accept it as we go

Who Am I

When you travel across this nation
do you walk the streets with pride
Do you think of all the value
you have built up deep inside

When you introduce yourself
do you say that my name is >>>>>>
or do you say I am _____,
because you're proud of this

You'll find there are many takers
less givers along the way
Noble men who walk this land
with honor and a God to pray

Can you be of noble character
and work each day to improve
Explore your soul and check yourself
so that others' lives will be moved

Can you say " I am a noble man,
I live the life the best I can,"
With respected honor and all my trust
this standard is a daily must

You'll become a man at eighteen
and go to work each day
You'll need to build the character
as life goes on its way

When you think you've gotten there
living a life of faith honor and deed
You'll need to daily check yourself
to fulfill this noble creed

For to become noble
each day you'll have the need
To search your soul for truthfulness
sew your honor with good deed

It is then that your will join the club
of great men laid to rest
Who sacrificed themselves
to provide our happiness

As angels they'll walk with you
and light the Earth's pathway
Help you plant your seed in life
before you pass away

We Poets

Twas a leaf that blew across my path
and made me stop and think
What is our purpose here with this gifted art
and a sea of poetic ink

Are we here to heal our wounded souls
or to touch another's heart
Putting words on paper
from whence we know not where they start

The churning caldron with in us
emits colossal feelings to display
Bringing forth emotions
in lives of disarray

A poet lives in all of us
feelings yet to be discovered
The beauty of the written word
often never gets uncovered

Jerrel E. Wolfe

But when there is a setback
tough times for you and me
Look inside your heart - for the artist
and the lucid poetry

www.ingramcontent.com/pod-product-compliance
Lightning Source LLC
LaVergne TN
LVHW040156080526
838202LV00042B/3187